Mishearing

By the same author

Poetry

To Thalia

On Reflection

Watermark

Open Water (Audio CD)

Phantom Limb

Concrete Tuesday

Anatomy of Voice

Numb & Number

Numb & Number (Audio CD)

Selected Poems

Fiction

Glissando

The Obituary Collector

Non-Fiction

Grotesque Anatomies: Menippean Satire Since the Renaiisance

Edited

Contemporary Australian Poetry (with M. Langford, J. Beveridge & J. Johnson)

Feeditng the Ghost 1: Criticism on Contemporary Australian Poetry (with A. Kissane and C. Rickett)

Mishearing

David Musgrave

Gorilla Books

First published in 2023
Published by Gorilla Books
7 Florabella Street
Warrimoo NSW 2774

info@gorillabooks.com

A catalogue record for this book is available from The National Library of Australia.

ISBN 9780645801903

Cover design by Matthew Holt

Printed by Lightning Source International

Contents

Preface

The poems in this book begin and end in myth. Their genesis was of the same moment that gave rise to *Anatomy of Voice* (2016): the desire to elegise a father, whether actual or literary, requires a stepping into myth, yet the subect of the poems of that earlier collection is voice. The realization of a voice is what allows us the means by which the operation of the imagination identifies the human with the non-human world; in other words it is the entry point into myth. This book, therefore, completes a circle begun with *Anatomy of Voice*, the composition of which began in late 2005.

As I explain in the introductory essay, these poems began as 'misheard' versions of other poems, my own and others'. Many poems, or drafts of poems, were created over nearly two decades, and the suite presented in this book is a selection of what I think are the most interesting results. There is no particular program to the selection of the original models other than that their voices struck me as distinctive in some way. In two instances I provide the source poem as well as its misheard version. Copyright issues, and an imperfect memory in some cases, prevent me from including the others.

Voice and Mishearing in Poetry

For a long time I have been preoccupied with the role that voice plays in our reception and understanding of poetry. By 'voice' I do not merely mean the performance or transmission of poetry by the human voice, but rather voice in the broadest sense that means style, or signature, but including those aspects of style which are traditionally the domain of stylometry, such as the distribution of frequently used words, as well as the less well-defined aspect of style that might be tentatively termed 'phonemic patterning'. The latter has been the subject of extensive studies since the time of Saussure's studies of anagrams in Saturnian verse, and it is this sonic distinctiveness that I largely want to focus on in this essay, and in the Mishearing suite. Is there a discernible correlation between distinctive sound patterning and authorship? The full answer to this question ultimately lies beyond the scope of this study, but the examples I use to consider what 'phonemic patterning' may consist of will, I hope, help to lay a framework for future thinking into this area. Despite the relevance of psychoanalytic approaches to considerations of voice (for example, Dolar, 2006), I will for the most part avoid speculating on this aspect, for space does not permit, and it is perhaps an issue to be addressed after the work of this book is done. Specifically, I will be addressing the question of what has been termed homophonic translation as an analog practice, with regard to my poems 'Coastline' and those contained in the second partition of *Anatomy of Voice*, as well as digitally (with a strong analog component) with regard to experiments with speech recognition in the Mishearing suite.

The Mishearing project utilises the speech recognition functionality of Microsoft Word 2003 to effect a form of homophonic translation of certain poems, with the view to seeing how the 'recognition' of speech via the mapping of phonemes to words bears a trace of the voice of the poet in the manner outlined above. That is, can the phonemic patterning of a poem remain recognisable after homophonic translation effected by imperfect speech recognition? The poems from the Mishearing project I will consider in this article are Dorothea Mackellar's 'My Country' and Seamus Heaney's 'To Pablo Neruda in Tamlaghtduff'. Before I can examine these examples of 'Mishearing' in detail, I will further explore what phonemic patterning is, following the example of Starobinski's engagement with Saussure's study of anagrams and Jakobson's further engagement with both in his studies of Shakespeare, Xlebnikov and folkloric riddles. I will further consider the notion of patterning as a distinct marker of an authorial selection from language considered from the point of view of words, as well as sounds chosen from those available in any given language. First of all, I will consider what is involved in homophonic translation.

What is 'homophonic translation'?

'Homophonic translation' is a term used in a variety of contexts ranging from analytic philosophy to experimental practices such as Celia and Louis Zukofsky's *Catullus* (Zukofsky, 1991), to the mondegreen and simple paronomasia. All of these are relevant to the Mishearing project, but there are differences between the way in which homophonic translation is understood in the analytic philosophical tradition, as is evident in Quine's collection of essays *Ontological Relativity and Other Essays* (Quine, 1969), and the way in which homophonic translation has been taken up as a tradition deriving from Zukofsky and others (including various members of Oulipo) in the Australian avant-garde by Chris Edwards, John Tranter and Toby Fitch. In the context of discussing the inscrutability of reference (Glock, 1993), Quine cites the hypothetical example of 'radical translation', meaning 'translation from a remote language on behavioral evidence, unaided by prior dictionaries' but concedes that in his argument 'the resort to a remote language was not really essential' and that 'radical translation begins at home' (Quine, 1969, p. 45). He continues:

> Must we equate our neighbor's English words with the same strings of phonemes in our own mouths? Certainly not; for sometimes we do not thus equate them. Sometimes we find it to be in the interests of communication to recognize that our neighbor's use of some word, such as 'cool' or 'square' or 'hopefully' differs from ours, and so we translate that word of his into a different string of phonemes in our idiolect. Our usual domestic rule of translation

is indeed the homophonic one, which simply carries each string of phonemes into itself; but still we are always prepared to temper homophony with what Neil Wilson has called the 'principle of charity'.[1] We will construe a neighbor's word heterophonically now and again if thereby we see our way to making his message less absurd. (Quine, 1969, p. 46)

And he goes on: 'The homophonic rule is a handy one on the whole … Homophonic translation is implicit in this social method of learning [e.g., imitating elders]. Departure from homophonic translation in this quarter would only hinder communication' (Quine, 1969, p. 46). Here we see that for Quine, homophonic translation is a model for communication and learning, yet in terms of communication involving different frames of reference, which could be understood to operate in both a synchronic and a diachronic sense, heterophonic translation is occasionally necessary.

Quine's notion of heterophonic translation bears some similarity to the term 'homophonic translation' as utilised by those who, following Zukofsky and various members of Oulipo, render words from a source language different to the target language based on similarity of sounds. The claims for what this kind of homophonic translation achieves range from Horáček's statement that the Zukofskys' *Catullus* 'dismantles the concept of transparent literalism as a foundation of fluency-based approaches to translation' and 'never abandons semantic correspondence but rather redefines it' (Horáček, 2014), to Bernstein's advocacy for homolinguistic and homophonic translations as means of writing a poem (Bernstein, 2021), and to Tranter's admission that, in his poem 'Desmond's Coupé', which is a 'homophonic' translation of Stéphane Mallarmé's 'Un Coup de dés':

> Though there are some tenuous links to the master poem, the employment of homophonic 'translation' causes the vocabulary and topic to vary erratically, leaping from seriousness to crude slang in a single phrase: 'heroic' to 'cough', for example. The only literary decorum is a total lack of decorum, relentlessly imposed. (Tranter, 2009, p. 121)

Another view of homophonic or mistranslation espoused by Toby Fitch emphasises the element of chance as well as the dethroning of meaning:

> Mistranslation in poetry, according to many experimenting or procedural poets [...] is a means to an end, a constraint-based, generative practice, whereby a poet 'translates' another poem (usually from a foreign language) into something *newly mistaken*. Transposition from one mode to another, as a practice/praxis, shortcircuits control, bringing chance to the fore – the poet is at the whim of words and their swervings. To double-up (or doubledown) on Walter Benjamin's 'Translation is a mode', let's think of mistranslation – predicated on ceding the initiative to a pre-text – as a *mood* 'in which meaning has ceased to be the watershed for the flow of language and the flow of revelation'. (Fitch, 2018, p. 17)

The desire to overturn, to thumb one's nose at sense, perhaps needs to be taken at face value as light-heartedness and fun; however, the claim that the process is aleatory, is a confusion of chance with contingency, as I have written about elsewhere (Musgrave, 2021, p. 175). At best, Fitch's notion of short-circuiting control can be understood as the source language serving as a kind of constraint against which the wit of the poet-translator is exercised. In the case of mistranslation, the poet is not really 'at the whim of words and their swervings' but rather makes selections, constrained by an apparent similarity to the phonemes of the source language, from language in a manner that has a significant unconscious element. Of course, unlike speech, where individual selections and arrangements of language are made in real time without full cognitive awareness, the process of writing, and of mistranslation, offers the opportunity for revision and invention. As an exercise in wit, such mistranslation has value, and the best example of it in the Australian tradition is Chris Edwards' mistranslation of Stéphane Mallarmé's 'Un coup de dés', 'A Fluke' (Edwards, 2005).

In distinction to the Australian avant-garde tradition of mistranslation, which is radically heterophonic in the Quinian sense, the Mishearing project has its basis in homophonic translation within the same language but is heterophonic in the sense that phonemes are 'misheard' by the speech recognition software, and the output resembles the source poem in shape and sound, but not (entirely) in sense.[2] We could term this kind of mistranslation 'hetero-homophonic' as it operates in one sense at the level of difference and offers the same possibilities as heterophonic mistranslation for the exercise of wit through revision and editing, while also perhaps evincing an element of parody; yet it also shares elements of homophonic translation with its basis in similarity of sound, and the occasional 'survival' of sounds from the original text in the 'misheard' version. Additionally, hetero-homophonic mistranslation raises interesting questions with regard to the translation of phonemic patternings, and whether these can be said to retain a sense of the voice of the original. This begs the question, of course, of the relation between voice as I have defined it above as a stylistic signature consisting of the patterning of keywords, which is the domain of stylometry, and the patterning of phonemes, which has been investigated by Saussure, Jakobson and others but is yet, to my knowledge, to be subject to stylometric analysis.

Before investigating phonemic patterning further, I want to briefly outline the method of production of the poems in the Mishearing suite. Microsoft Word 2003 has a native speech recognition function, by default trained to a North American accent. I avoided the 'training' process of attuning the software to an Australian accent, and I used a microphone of poor quality, held at different distances from my mouth and occasionally muffled by a tissue or a cloth, and the recordings took place in the presence of varying degrees of ambient noise. From experience, the software appears to reference Word's in-built dictionary, Microsoft Outlook's personal folders and cached web pages to map sounds to words, using probabilistic tables in a manner similar to that of stylometric programs such as 'Stylo' and the textual analysis/reconstruction program 'Brekdown'. I would repeat the process a number of times for a single poem using different combinations of distance, bafflement, and ambient noise, and then set about producing a single version through selection and some editing. The result, in deference to Tranter's experiments with

'Brekdown', is given a name that is an anagram of the original poem title. Thus Dorothea Mackellar's 'My Country' becomes 'Cymru Tony', Judith Wright's 'Wildflower Plain' becomes 'Low Ripe Windfall', Les Murray's 'Spring Hail' becomes 'Lip Sharing', Gig Ryan's 'The Cross/The Bay', becomes 'Be the Scary Host', and a passage from *Finnegans Wake*, 'Genie Wanks Fan'.

Mishearing and information theory

In his book *Auditory Scene Analysis: The Perceptual Organization of Sound*, Albert S Bregman cites the research of O'Leary and Rhodes into phonemic restoration, whereby a subject listens to a recording of speech that is interrupted by periodic silent gaps, apparently finding that 'filling the gaps by noise can actually improve the accuracy of recognition' (Bregman, 1994, p. 376). Bregman goes on to ask:

> Why should this be? After all, the nervous system cannot supply information that is missing from the stimulus. It can only supply its best guess. Why could it not do that without the noise filling the gap? I have argued earlier that the noise eliminates false transitions from sound to silence and vice versa that are interfering with the recognition of the sounds.[3] In addition, because silences are interpreted as part of the speech itself and not as an added sound, the rhythmic introduction of silences is heard as a rhythm in the speech itself and disrupts the listener's perception of any natural rhythms that may have been in the original speech.[4]
>
> The method of repeatedly interrupting a stream of speech has been used to show how the restorations depend on being able to develop a guess about the deleted sound from a consideration of the other nearby words. (Bregman, 1994, p. 376)

Silence, therefore, is both a necessary signifying part of speech and also its antithesis. The introduction of noise would seem to minimise the uncertainty as to whether the introduced silences were signifying or non-signifying. In terms of the Mishearing project's use of speech-recognition, distance, bafflement and ambient noise would function in the same way, with this important proviso: if a listener is able to accurately guess missing sounds from their context, it means that the remaining phonemes possess some kind of information about those missing parts. Here we are getting closer to what the Mishearing project may in part be revealing to us: the probabilistic nature of certain sound patterns, and the possibility that traditional stylometry (for example, Stylo, Brekdown, Verse by Verse), which tracks the deep and occluded process of individuation in language selection and arrangement at the level of the word, can be used to track individuation in phonemic selection and patterning, thus complementing our understanding of authorial distinctiveness through word patterning with the patterning of sound as well. It goes without saying that this process is inherently meaningful in hetero-homophonic translation in the same language, more so than hetero-homophonic translation across different languages.

At this point it might be worth countenancing the objection that to mishear is to mistake, and there is nothing more to be said on the matter. But the thing about the human voice is that it originates in the body and, when heard, ends in another. In an age where AIs such as ChatGPT or Google's Verse by Verse can write poetry and programs such as Neil Rubenking's 'Brekdown' can combine the poetry of one poet with the style of another, is the voice that inessential part of a poem which, when lost, takes the author with it? Certainly, John Tranter thought so when he asked the question:

> How does a writer create a writer-free literary text? A text free of authorial intentions and without buried cultural, social, economic and political values and hidden personality agendas, giving forth only 'literature' in its pure state? (Tranter, 1998)

I am not that sure such purity is at all possible, even if Tranter meant it ironically. In terms of the digital transmission of a message, uncertainty is resolved completely once a message has been successfully received, having been homophonically translated through space and time. In the analog environment, it is a little different: strings of phonemes, which travel as sound waves through the air, cause vibrations of the tympanum, which in turn set off movements in the auditory ossicles – that tiny forge where the malleus, incus and stapes work to transmit to the cochlea, filled with endolymph – where the mechanical movements are transduced into neural impulses. Hearing is therefore a transcription of sorts, and as such cannot ever be said to be perfect, for there is energy lost through the act of aural transcription of the message in the air, and in the middle and inner ears. In addition to the physical imprecision of hearing, there is the potential to mis-listen in the homophonic translation of homonyms and the heterophonic translation of unfamiliar words.

In each of these models I have just sketched, it is assumed that the phoneme has no signifying force in itself, only in a string of phonemes. This is a view shared by most 20th century philosophers of language; for example, Giorgio Agamben writes 'the phoneme is singularly close to the Heideggerian idea of a "voice without sound" and of a "sound of silence"' (Agamben, 1991, p. 86). This view of the phoneme is a 20th century phenomenon and is best exemplified by Jakobson's view that '"A phoneme", as Sapir remarked, "has no singleness of reference". All phonemes denote nothing but mere OTHERNESS' (Jakobson & Halle, 2002, p. 22). However, it is well worth noting that in the second half of the 19th century, the term had currency in psychiatry as an auditory hallucination (an interesting fact to which I shall return):

> Phonemes (the verbal auditory hallucinations of Séglas) have a special significance, inasmuch as they consist of 'words representing ideas' (Rogues de Fursac, 1905, i 44);
>
> The more complicated hallucinations which are conceived by the patient to be 'voices' – verbal auditory hallucinations – are known as phonemes (White, 1911, 47);

Jakobson explains that within phonemics, the phoneme is as an irreducible, non-signifying 'particle', an invariant 'building block' analogous to the atom of physics. He acknowledges that this is a relatively recent development, and is also anxious to trace its pre-history:

> The search for the ultimate discrete differential constituents of language can be traced back to the *sphoṭa*-doctrine of the Sanskrit grammarians and to Plato's conception of στοιχεῖον, but the actual linguistic study of these invariants started only in the 1870's and developed intensively after World War I, side by side with the gradual expansion of the principle of invariance in the sciences. (Jakobson & Halle, 2002, pp. 18-19)

While this kind of thought is typical of the development of the social sciences through the 20th century (Midgley, 2001), there are other ways of considering the phoneme. For example, recent research suggests that the relation between certain sounds and words are not entirely arbitrary (Blasi et al, 2016; Dingemanse et al, 2015; Griffiths, 2011; Monaghan et al, 2014).[5] Even if these relatively recent findings are found to be questionable, we have seen that Bregman has suggested the possibility that phonemes contain information about other phonemes, and Jakobson – in discussing the likelihood that 'it is possible from a part of the sequence [of phonemes] to predict with greater or lesser accuracy the succeeding features, to reconstruct the preceding ones, and finally to infer from some features in a bundle the other concurrent features' (Jakobson & Halle, 2002, p. 16) – seems to be suggesting the same. These observations can be explained by classic information theory, in which the measure of information in a system is understood as a logarithmic relation of uncertainty, or Shannon entropy (Shannon, 1948). A system of phonemes is informational in this sense, even if each phoneme is non-signifying. And the information of a phonemic system can be comprised of several things: the rules of a language that permit or forbid certain phonemes and their combinations; the possibility that certain idiolects or dialects favour certain phonemes; the possibility that the individual's selection of words, which we know from stylometry is distinctive, may be governed by the sounds of those words, or even by a preference for certain sounds (sometimes over sense); and lastly, the self-conscious selection of words and sounds by poets when composing poetry, which is never entirely without a subliminal aspect. This last possibility has received extensive attention from linguists, with Saussure and Jakobson being two prominent exemplars. In his book on Saussure's anagrams, Starobinski writes of the transmission of legends across centuries that:

> … one must consider meaning as a product – the variable product of the combinative function [of the material elements of a legend] – and not as a preliminary absolute, *ne varietur.*
>
> In Poetry it is clear that the laws of usage are concerned not only with verbal unities ('concepts invested with linguistic form') and with symbols; the phonemes themselves are used according to specific laws. And these laws can vary, depending on style, period, tradition. (Starobinski, 1979, pp. 8-9)

I will examine this attention to the phonemes themselves in the work of Saussure and Jakobson in the following section, in order to prepare the ground for the discussion of individually distinctive sound patterning in the Mishearing suite.

Subliminal verbal patterning in poetry

From 1906 to 1909, Ferdinand de Saussure devoted over one hundred notebooks to the phenomenon of anagrams in, initially, Latin Saturnian verse, and subsequently in poetry from several periods, including Vedic poetry, medieval French poetry and German poetry. He claimed to have discovered a rule by which a hypogram, or concealed name or theme-word (in the case of Saturnian verse, the name of the individual memorialised in the poem; in other poems, either the hero or title) is then rearranged in successive lines according to set rules.[6] As Starobinski notes:

> The hypogram inserts a simple name into the complex array of syllables in a poetic line; its function will be to recognize and reassemble its leading syllables, as Isis reassembled the dismembered body of Osiris. (Starobinski, 1979, p. 20)[7]

The problem which Saussure was unable to overcome was his doubt that these paragrammatic and anagrammatic identifications were not, in fact, apophenic, a problem exacerbated by the fact that he was able to apply his rules and make identifications seemingly at will. Starobinski is of the opinion that Saussure refrained from publication because he could not resolve these questions, and indeed Saussure confesses at one point that 'everything overlaps, and one cannot see where to draw the line' (Starobinski, 1979, p. 98). What becomes apparent in reading through Starobinski's selections from Saussure's notebooks is an anxiety accompanied by frustration that certainty cannot be found in his hypothesis. Yet there is also an awareness that, in Starobinski's words:

> Ferdinand de Saussure interprets classical poetry as an art of *combination*, whose developed structures are tributaries of simple elements, fundamentals which are required by the rules of the game to be both conserved and transformed. Only it happens that all language is combination, even without the intervention of an explicit intention to practice combination as art. Decipherers, whether they be cabalists or phoneticists, have a free range: a reading which is symbolic or numeric or systematically attentive to a partial aspect can always bring to light a latent depth, a hidden secret, a language within the language. And if there is no cipher? The constant attraction of the secret, of anticipated discovery, of steps astray in the labyrinth of exegesis – all these would remain. (Starobinski, 1979, p. 129)

It is worth noting that 'the *Course in General Linguistics*, developed between 1907 and 1911, is in large part of a later date than the research into anagrams' (Starobinski, 1979, p. x) and that the anxiety over the ungrounded combination of phonemes was retained and transferred to a more generalised fear of the system of language as he had come to theorise it.[8] Starobinski's recuperation of Saussure's studies into anagrams was taken up by several linguists and scholars of style, including Roman Jakobson, who seems relatively untroubled by Saussure's apophenic fears. For example, in his essay 'Subliminal Verbal Patterning in Poetry' he finds the titular hero of Xlebnikov's poem 'The Grasshopper' to be embedded anagrammatically in its lines, while the answer to a folkloric riddle can also be found in a manner similar to what he calls Saussure's 'daring studies on poetic anagrams' (Jakobson, 1985, p. 61). In his study of Shakespeare's 'Sonnet 129' he finds a crucial anagrammatic insertion of Shakespeare's own name (as well as in sonnets 134-136 and 76). For Jakobson, these anagrams are part and parcel of the poet's intuition which:

> ... may act as the main or, not seldom, even sole designer of the complicated phonological and grammatical structures in the writings of individual poets. Such structures, particularly powerful on the subliminal level, can function without any assistance of logical judgement and patent knowledge both in the poet's creative work and in its perception by the sensitive reader. (Jakobson, 1985, p. 68)

We know that subliminal verbal patterning is what stylometric analysis has succeeded in establishing as individual authorial signature styles based on patterns in common word choice. It is my contention that stylometric analysis of phonetic units would succeed in uncovering other patterns, equally distinctive and that these, taken together with common word choice patterns would approximate voice as I have defined it; moreover, it would help us to understand that voice in poetry is what sits at the juncture of conservation and transformation.

From rhyme to hypogram: *Anatomy of Voice*

'The willed production of sound always is in tension with the involuntary aspect of hearing,' writes Susan Stewart in her essay 'Rhyme and Freedom', and she continues: 'in rhyme, the production of sound can seem involuntary and hearing can be attuned to particular intervals' (Stewart, 2009, p. 41). In many ways, rhyme was my portal into the Mishearing project, with years spent before it reading the slant rhymes of Paul Muldoon, which owe much to the poetry of Louis MacNeice, among others. The rhyming of 'rickshaw' with 'peepshow', for example, in MacNeice's 'Bagpipe Music' or the slant rhyme of the title of Muldoon's little poem about alcoholism, 'The Mist-Net', with the last line '*You mustn't. You mustn't.*' caught my ear as much for their chiming imperfection as for their subtle structuration (MacNeice, 2001, p. 32; Muldoon, 2001, p. 156). Stewart is right to defend the inclusion of rhyme in one's poetic armory as an endowment 'with certain freedoms',

> among them: the vernacular, including the locality of the poem itself, released from the standard; the monolingual in dialogue with the multilingual; sound opened up by vision, and sound released from meaning entirely; expectation released into surprise; and pattern drawn from the oblivion of time. (Stewart, 2009, p. 48)

When Stewart writes of 'sound released from meaning entirely', she is referring to semantics, but there are other meanings which are not linguistic which structured sound contains, such as musicality, and the intimation of an order that may be beyond words, as well as aesthetic concerns: distaste, for those poets and readers who abhor rhyme, pleasure for those who do not.

My initial response to these various considerations of rhyme and its variants was to adopt, as a constraint, the rearrangement of the terminal phonemes of rhyming lines, which in practice involved up to four syllables and which also involved the occasional inversion of phonemes. The result was the poem 'Coastline', in which sonorousness arose from a process of fracture. The next step was to extend the process of manually rearranging terminal phonemes to those that comprised an entire line. In the second partition of *Anatomy of Voice,* I took each line of a nine-line poem and, in order, used them as the first lines of nine subsequent poems, each of which had six lines, with the second to sixth lines consisting of rearrangements of the phonemes making up the first line. Here is the fourth of these rearranged poems, with accompanying image:

Conjured from nothing but parts of the flesh.
In your pungent rhumbas, the shuffle of
injured tongues. From the *book-trap* of shelf
the jury thronged the prefab muff confits.
Bud Junior, of shopping tube country, films
the pledge of neuro-buffing comfort shunts.

The motto for this image is '*Tamen Discam*', which can be translated as 'Let me learn', and is taken from Gabriel Rollenhagen's *Nucleus*, Arnheim, 1611. I Nr. 75. Its accompanying verses:

> Et licet in tumbam pes decidat alter, et alter
> Vivat adhuc, studiis invigilabo tamen
>
> [Although one foot might fall into the tomb, and the other
>
> might go on still living, yet I shall pay close attention to my studies]
>
> (Henkel, 1996, p. 982; Musgrave, 1996, p. 97)

are a laudation of learning. The intention here was, coincidentally, very close to the 'rules' which Saussure discerned in Saturnian verse: I wanted to see what anagrams such rearrangement would yield and to see if one of these anagrams could serve as a 'key' (which I then indicated in italics) that could correspond to an image from one of several thousand emblems dating from the fifteenth through to the eighteenth centuries which embodied one of the virtues of Bill Maidment, my late friend. In this regard, phonemic rearrangement was an artistic practice animated by grief. I have written elsewhere about this:

> I hit upon the idea of the emblem as something which might convey a personal quality as much as a conventional moral. Those emblems I have included in the book were chosen for the way in which they seemed to embody many of Bill's virtues, but were also chosen for the way in which they arose, often seemingly by chance, from the poems I was composing. The Second Partition could be considered as a small emblem book in its own right. (Musgrave, 2016, p. 92)

The hypogram does not arise by chance for, as with apophenia in general, *something* will arise, or appear, from the process of looking or, in this case, rearranging something as apparently fundamental and inconsequential as the phoneme. It was nevertheless a pleasing part of the overall design of *Anatomy of Voice*, not the least because the operation at the level of the phoneme seemed to bear some trace of that word's original meaning of 'auditory hallucination' (noted above): 'Phonemes (the verbal auditory hallucinations of Séglas) have a special significance, inasmuch as they consist of "words representing ideas"' (Rogues de Fursac, 1905, 44); 'The more complicated hallucinations which are conceived by the patient to be "voices" – verbal auditory hallucinations – are known as phonemes' (White, 1911, 47); especially fitting, given the genesis of *Anatomy of Voice* was in just such an auditory hallucination (Musgrave, 2016, p. 93).

The Mishearing suite

The following are two examples of misheard poems from the Mishearing suite, accompanied by their originals. I undertake a reading of them after Ross Chambers' notion of 'paratextual density' (2018).

'My Country'

The love of field and coppice
Of green and shaded lanes,
Of ordered woods and gardens
Is running in your veins.
Strong love of grey-blue distance,
Brown streams and soft, dim skies
I know, but cannot share it,
My love is otherwise.

I love a sunburnt country,
A land of sweeping plains,
Of ragged mountain ranges,
Of droughts and flooding rains.
I love her far horizons,
I love her jewel-sea,
Her beauty and her terror
The wide brown land for me!
(Mackellar, 1987, p. 11)

'Cymru Tony'

The love of this agreement
chided lines before the words
and ideas running new times
strong loss of a great lady
stands for streams and soft team skies
and I became a share
my love is otherwise

allow the Sunday country land
is sweeping kinds of writing
and running shoes of transit
funding Ryan's love

is the rise of some of the jewels
say the PC and that era
the profit from a stock swap

The voice of Dorothea Mackellar's 'My Country' ('Cymru Tony'[9]) strikes me as blunt and earnest. The vowels are short and repetitive ('love', 'sun', 'count'), and where they are apposed to the longer vowels ('sweeping', 'far'), the contrast is heightened by the connotation of the sounds and words contained by those words with the longer vowels: 'Sweeping' contains 'weep', and 'wee', 'far' contains the 'ah' of a cry of pain, 'terror' contains 'error' or 'err'. One interesting feature of the Mishearing project in general is the prevalence of numbers, proper nouns and language relating to economic activity generally in the misheard version, suggestive of some generalised pecuniary anxieties or preoccupations.

'My Country' was published in a collection titled *The Closed Door* in 1911, the title implying that secrets were contained within, perhaps requiring decoding. Michael Farrell's reading of Mackellar's poem draws attention to its title which 'enacts settler identification and possession' (Farrell, 2015, p. 87), and his discussion of Mackellar's writing generally focuses upon her secret diary, which was written using an invented code. What is the relation between the voice of this famous poem and this elaborate concealment? According to Farrell, 'Mackellar is more concerned to hide her desires, and their intensity, rather than her actions' although ultimately he sees that the *Diaries*' 'value is the critique they offer of the settlement model' (Farrell, 2015, pp. 88, 91). Certainly, a reading which focusses on unsettlement in the diaries raises the question of whether this effect is entirely absent from 'My Country', or whether the poem indeed helps produce 'a home or settled structure' in relation to Australia's national culture' (Farrell, 2015, p. 96). It is significant, perhaps, that the line 'my love is otherwise' survives hetero-homophonic translation; in doing so it draws attention to itself and offers ways in which it may be read, as 'other than wise', or foolish. And certainly, the overwrought love affair with R. (Brisbane-based architect Robin Dods) implies an attraction to drama and the need to hide it, but there are also numerous diary entries referring to heavy menstruation (Farrell, 2015, p. 89). Perhaps the sounds of pain concealed in 'My Country' emerge in its misheard version as a softened commodification of desire; certainly 'running', 'streams' and 'transit' figure prominently in the misheard first two stanzas.

To Pablo Neruda in Tamlaghtduff

Niall Fitzduff brought a jar
of crab-applejelly
made from crabs off the tree
that grew at Duff's corner –
still grows at Duff's Corner –
a tree I never once saw
with crab apples on it.

Contrary, unflowery
sky-whisk and bristle, more
twig-fret than fruit-fort,
crabbed
as crabbed could be –
that was the tree
I remembered.
(Heaney, 2006, p. 64)

Did Unfathomable Flagrant Pout

Nil fits a lot tougher a
bridge at this critical jelly
made from grapes off the tree
that growing doubts corner
still grows it does: the country
and never once always credible
song that contrary to unflattering
skyways can bristle more quick

for it than for it for granted script
could be a thought was that rehire
amended

In his review of *District and Circle*, Brad Leithauser notes that Heaney's 'rhymes are rough-hewn, hand-honed' and that his 'harmonies have grown harsher over time' (Leithauser, 2006). Certainly, roughening is one of the markers of late style (Jones, 2010, pp. 1-9), and in Heaney's poem the mix of fricative and labial is a kind of bluff verbal biffo. It's a certainty of voice that strikes, with compound words neatly morticing characteristic Heaney sounds, the guttural 'r' that confidently places the poem in the local, the district, a poetic world a million miles away. These compound words are compressed versions of the rough rhymes of which Leithauser asks:

> What does it matter? Why should we care whether two words chime cleanly or clunkily? The issue can seem picayune – until you recognize that it's through just such tiny touches, such minimal modifications of sound, that a poet fabricates an individual, distinguishing music. (Leithauser, 2006)

At first pass, the poem seems confidently nostalgic, exuding the kind of poetic authority one might expect when one Nobel laureate includes another in his poem. There is also, as so often in Heaney, the confident use of Irish language, proper nouns and names, all of which ring authentically as local, and rural: it reads as almost the exact antithesis of John Tranter's suite of poems about literary thinkers in Sydney pubs (Tranter, 1990, pp. 149-153). But when the poem is misheard, an interesting translation takes place: 'Duff' becomes 'doubt', and lines 6-7 become 'never once always credible / song'. Reading the two poems paratextually, we return to Heaney's poem and notice that the crab-apple jelly comes from Niall Fitzduff, and that the crabs grow on Duff's corner: the poem is literally 'up the duff' with crabs; yet there are other senses too, of duff: that it means to steal goods by changing their appearance. Is that what we make of Neruda's presence in Tamlaghtduff, that Heaney has stolen from the Chilean Nobel laureate by changing the appearance, in translation of his words? The crabs themselves transport the persona of Heaney's poem back to a past which has its own 'crab-hoard', a crowded irritability brought on by the speaker's crabbed, sideways translation into the fantasised presence of the Chilean poet, replete with verbal invention that reads partly as homage, partly as anxiety of the inescapable influence, perhaps of the older poet.

Subliminally, I think, Heaney's sound choices reveal an uncertainty; whether it is due to the onset of a late style, or an anxiety of influence, a 'rehire / amended'. Here it is relevant to consider Ross Chambers' notion of paratextual density in looking at the ways I have read the misheard versions against their sources:

> Thanks to all these devices, then – the in-built redundancy of natural languages, the specific modes of redundancy that produce the 'poetic function' of language, and finally the 'kinds' of transaction that are defined by the working of genre – the artful texts that we call literary resist entropy and through densification survive the effect of time with considerable success. The type of intertextuality that defines the relation of 'L'Invitation au Voyage' and 'Grab Your Passport' as a matter of mutual replication or paraphrase produces a kind of density, or thickening, that further intensifies the negentropic *Dichtung* that puts literature in general, and poetry in particular, on the side of life in humanity's long battle against time and the work of death. And that is the case even when its themes may incorporate a death-wish or some other form of 'degeneracy' (the sort of thing Tranter attributes to Baudelaire in his paratextual note). Like sexual congress, textual congress works for life against death; and it does so even unto death – which is, of course, the ultimate significance of the *Liebestod*. (Chambers, 2018, p. 235)

In Chambers' understanding, the readings I have offered with regard to these two misheard poems might best be seen as aspects of the paratextual 'thickening' that occurs between the misheard and its original.

In this regard, the Mishearing project is, ultimately, yet one more way to achieve that densification and resistance of entropy to which Chambers refers, although Chambers is mixing his frames of reference here, using 'entropy' in the quotidian sense of decay and disorder, rather than the sense of it as a measure of the information of a system, according to classic information theory. In the latter sense, the Mishearing project is concerned with increasing the amount of entropy in the text, or at least between the texts, for as I have shown in my brief examples, hetero-homophonic translation of the constituent phonemes reveals rather more in the texts than was there before. And it is a first, analog step in helping to identify phonemic pattering in poetry and to identify the distinctiveness of a poetic voice.

Conclusion

Perhaps the best stylometric analysis is that which poets intuit in their bones, about their own work and that of others. Mackellar's phonemic patterning is in blunt triads apposed to longer vowel sounds revealing suffering and uncertainty. Heaney's style in *District and Circle* is indeed 'late' (when compared, say, with a sample from *Death of a Naturalist*) and is crabbed and guttural. And yet, it is distinctly possible that my mishearings of both poems possess elements of my own style.

As stated at the outset, I have deliberately avoided any discussion of the psychoanalytic aspects of voice, but like anything repressed, it returns at the end to haunt us, like a missing transcendental signifier, or Saussure's terror at its absence. The subliminal ordering of words and sounds can reveal aspects of desire, but it can equally be argued to reveal the kinds of anxieties or 'unsettlement' which Farrell explores with Mackellar, and in Ned Kelly's 'Jerilderie letter (Farrell, 2015, pp. 48-53, 85-100). Mladen Dolar's *A Voice and Nothing More* contains a critique of Jakobson's fascination with *lalangue* (Dolar, 2006, pp. 145-149) and is rich with new possibilities. Adriana Cavarero's *For More than One Voice* is centred more on a 'politics of the voice', and it seems to me that one consequence of renewed attention to the distinctiveness of voice is an understanding and allowing of pluralism:

> Paying attention to the voice is acknowledging that a speaking voice only exists because it has a listener. In this regard there is a political dimension to identifying what is characteristic in a voice understood as 'a vocal exchange where the repetition of sound, and all its tonal rhythmic variants, expose uniqueness as an understanding [*un'intesa*] and a reciprocal dependence.' (Cavarero, 2005, p. 182)

After all, the voice's first function after birth is to call to the other. In a literary sense, the development (or identification) of a voice is that which enables us to enter into the process of myth, understood as the operation of the imagination to identify the human with the non-human world (Frye, 1947, p. 19). As a portal into myth, voice occupies the juncture of conservation and transformation, making these efforts to understand its distinctiveness all the more important.

Yet for all of this renewed interest in the voice in poetry, and the various experiments described and detailed herein, perhaps the most important development in modern poetry took place in the early Jurassic, around 195 million years ago, with the appearance of Hadrocodium, a small mammaliaform, now extinct, approximately 3.2 cm long and possessing a nearly full mammalian ear. One cannot speculate how the evolution of mammals, let alone humans, might have occurred without the faculty of hearing, but it is certain that poetry would not exist without it.

Mishearing

Albo bling

We cut across available states
to the low end of the day
to attack an error
tying the ferry to tree-bones
and a Miles Davis CD
vendor found more influence in love
than loans of sunlight
schooled the show
dialed 'dragonfly' as drums,
statements, citizens say, 'July
ducks drift off the head of a currawong.'
Friends like to show
an angel as if trying not to belong
to those investments
and you said, 'this is kind of, like that's
five runs low,' and pointed
to a soft patch of lawn from Louis David
that comes with having changed the war
and a tangle of telling branches
into law
broken by some juice
called from lead paint
and the other waited for the perfect angle
to manage somehow.
Think actions as soon as a dragonfly,
that's the easy thing
you couple an intricate
'Hi, Shelley'
bush-based games
that surface for a while
then disappeared for feedlots,
minutes, the sun's long rise

into a shallow piece
to quit, and read of lives
the rise of the trial of one million spruiking
new wasps of the two branches of well-being.
Subway Z-3 was once the highway,
a report was fruitful into the long run,
the 6:30 am ride plunges and crops
the rooms of two million homes and lives.

Be the Scary Host

The chancellor of the three main audience cities
names the endless pariah state-paid recreation leap of pain.
She recalls infecting out nine
when the plane is made cosmetic,
the visited directions
when Stone is on the line.
The time, the region, price, of course,
like if you sink your pelvis.
He pitches for five dealers
and drops, in the thick of the lease, them.
All the corporate retreats on the status quo
in another flood of Spanish comment
sit still. See, a dialogue crumbs.
You recall on the crime scene, while waiting,
strong black flies, the CPU circuits, and it.

Connected Om Sigh

Kenny and any and the widening guy,
the Falcons can hear the Falcons.
Are things falling into the city?
He cannot hold Munich.
He's the one that will not be entirely slow,
used in every way to the ceremony of innocence.
It's true that this level of each and, while he was full of the
passionate intensity of Chile's senate elections,
is showing the second coming of the hand.
The second coming of the others would then set off Ostinga jackets.
This money troubles my son
and we're, in a sense, of the desert
and charges line body in the head of them
and you guys playing can people this.
Is the son moving his life as well to the ocean?
Is sixteen Dave's? And that's the doctor dropped again?
Until a knife and twenty centuries of study sleep with a text
not made by a rocky ride. And what broad-based outcome
it must slash toward this for him to be known?

The Second Coming

William Butler Yeats

Turning and turning in the widening gyre
The falcon cannot hear the falconer;
Things fall apart; the centre cannot hold;
Mere anarchy is loosed upon the world,
The blood-dimmed tide is loosed, and everywhere
The ceremony of innocence is drowned;
The best lack all conviction, while the worst
Are full of passionate intensity.

Surely some revelation is at hand;
Surely the Second Coming is at hand.
The Second Coming! Hardly are those words out
When a vast image out of Spiritus Mundi
Troubles my sight: somewhere in sands of the desert
A shape with lion body and the head of a man,
A gaze blank and pitiless as the sun,
Is moving its slow thighs, while all about it
Reel shadows of the indignant desert birds.
The darkness drops again; but now I know
That twenty centuries of stony sleep
Were vexed to nightmare by a rocking cradle,
And what rough beast, its hour come round at last,
Slouches towards Bethlehem to be born?

Medical

nine is a spear
was the city and in
gold is the awful link in the first time
watching
and the number of SAMS can be launched.
The client and the skewers in the polls that he's not
strolls in an old infantile snow
and saliva doubling
in from the rearing free market.
Now he's meant to be reaching his side-to-side,
looking into his head as luck would have it,
grown in loans to collect
and cleaning.

One rising up from the options and questions
that grants bill, that would connect,
and some holding their breaths and astonished
and love reading once more that line is that
from due death and live crew includes links from his time.
To respond to the smells
is the holding hands to the sanctions,
grain dog walker,
eighth and stock and see
the yeasty style was the Russians.
Are under-chances
warden months to own the team,
as my kid who was the mental institution?
Like none of these mountains
matadors will rise,
making line and a sea sand.

A Mute Spoof

Steering the monster remark
had difficulties to define just what
amounts to monstrosity in that area
would reappear in its native phenol fact
to the twin lives and die
in the general air of an imprint,
a saying the printers have spurned:
'the median is simply famous architects
of the mayonnaise of mass,'
if he wants to fist creation of those eyes.
For this, back the falcons.

Nothing.
Nothing there
but they had its tiny tuition
and the finish for a CIA,
just the slums in his chair like a badly hit man.
Half-life science is accused,
a rapist in that game and still changing
from tissue and follicles of a file.

The spirit electrical supports
the close of an old mile
or is that woman that race?
Bring it along with black drapery drums
and funeral train like a great man's call
from '99. He's not. Did that
in this true story house? Once the humiliation
of use in obscurity,
the orchard plight of a heavy ambition
trapped the fermenting of the yeasty heart
stopped best with such pyrotechnics

that all worlds gagged and repeat
that still might, but old peace efforts
to concoct the old heroic thing
from the money and prize from the parents
working into a nutshell…

From the banning of these reasons
by use of lifting
wrecked and monstrous services
to assist a consumer's lumbering,
obsolete arsenal of gigantic warplanes
from a time when half the world still burns.
Sad to blink behind it as an adult.

Cymru Tony

The love of this agreement
chided lines before the words
and ideas running new times.
Strong loss of a great lady
stands for streams and soft team skies
and I became a share:
my love is otherwise.

Allow the Sunday country land
is sweeping kinds of writing
and running shoes of transit.
Funding Ryan's love
is the rise of some of the jewels
say the PC and that era,
the profit from a stock swap.

Greenback forests won't read them
and the stuff I missed that mentions
the hot gold rush of new
clean single of the brushes
with lively all-in-all,
its stake to treat IDs and friends,
and that oil court might have.

My country competes in this place,
we see it happening, receiving cattle,
but in the quake last data
and we can place a game,
that running of the nineteen sixties,
I came running. Court might have
my country land of writing.

If I have my country,
land of the running back,
gold for flood and fire
and famine to buy a suspect
file the Defence Department
watch after many guys.
That only vial of green
begins this weekend –

Guy is an idler, had a country,
the title country will fall
on average land. You have not left
and it will not understand
how many splendours whenever
I might die, and to what brand
of country my timing phones will fly?

e-blab

Of this and that is more to say if I want it.
You will host a house
but he wants the nation,
so that leaves two princes.
Mid-seventies French is going well for justice.
It isn't that.
Just given domain to the classroom street,
wrote, 'back from the war with the missing
and the lost mind of the Portland cup
from Guildford.' Fell from untruths, we'll see
you really have to register. Two agencies
will be confined in the local and longstanding river
that needs to be said. Is constantly said.
Clearly signed by a multitude.
And nothing is said.

Lady Rightfist

This inches.
And forced breeding to the last of the family
shows that one always brings, shunning something,
which is the data on the United States,
of things in life with instructions
that, raised by the way sport was
once more inclined to us,
is that this fall's like an audience kind:
will remain plastic sheets.
They will we be lined up along the times
crucial for our problems,
shaken when the closing scene
in its moves is the familiar: seven tractors
and definitions of a feisty bond King
of the year after we invested so much in, what was every day
and pointed to the very thing and nothing.
Now we typeset the right alliance like competing colleagues
and double legends pretend
it's all just apply in the oven
this tight range with series wrapped around us
to get on, incredibly. To continue: no one gets to forty —
well, on to the farmhouse for that!
Without guns showing interested parties
what makes that,
I get a file.
A bullet concerns Gingrich.

Her Rivet

The steps I can-can,
and all the world's performing.

Not sexy styles hung in the Lybrand
using small fires

running wives of intimacy —
islands passing China made us

and a waste is patented talking.
My hands and a flying fox collided as much,

rocked the surface memory and phones,
rocks on show on a mailing list of five

and each extinguished stock and I
endorse information that I've a long drive.

The memory shaman's
fragments are falling into place

and the heavens for the eleventh time
reveal themselves as moderate trial dates

and it's between channel and shell
gathering in cosmic spindles, Milky Ways, a Gemini's

local dashboard of central around me.
She surrounds me, has locked me in speeches:

that butterfly exploiting himself, thrown over. The net supplies
the entrance fee to the Russian SEC.

Truth tiles have spread to happen
to own a gallon of my hair is mountainous, maintain a hundred and five,

like three separate invalids shifting before me in an age-old place infected
for motions, stocks, and others placed before may contain all the trees

and saying the next of the supplies, coming news is that either the yields
on themselves are later and fleet by $3.00 of sales rise breaking said

this pristine lot is watching memory from its original lineaments
to not times its onion

those joining a mango as the party
claim bodies play a mage and hands across time field fear

a chance to the monument of the fish,
and wins in a Span, waving from Iraq

hives of leniency step back
and my love for a long shot through with the seven

changes the memory as we face each other online
and it's now I get to its two of two centuries

almost a given an official decider to retain the rushing tie, the game
and be kind to each other but he fired the Cincinnati New Year between
swamplands

to tell it like a fourth of the world seemed to save the lives
and the Santa the tide to the river that cell and it is now I should

Ink is a good to a pricklet

After practice in the Philippines at Titan,
it's a title fighting guest enjoying ice cream:
Gerald 'the sunspot' Clinton.
He's first in,
this is the closest you ever get.
The same rates rising up the Chinese
that films on the side of appeal
has decided he unveils married couples.
Reflect all Switzerland on the job of oxygen status
and then let the ashtray
the Chiu in the third title fight
in gas asleep in the mail.
As dialog signing and all that talk city chat
and happy to breathe again like a revived its cries
we go fish
plus pages to the telephone survey areas
said 'beautiful' to loss of close friends like they do
through to the win the sun publishes
the wall as gold and invisible.
A million shared telegrams collapse in this night
while many in on the classic country: as we fly across the main
and after the piano jazz to sleep in a round
we wake up and it's a title fight
and guess that it might be your ship factory now.
I can tell in this way that the topics
because you have an issue
lose the green banks of the beta.

Lip Sharing

This is the spring which you may remember,
boil it down.
                    Harry,
we could fly all together for a long time
above the shootings and vanished koan wall
                 and then the hammering   *full on*

would seize the quivering Hanks
to the news of Mr. Draft   is that it can
money to the songs
                                that grew at this time
and that they had fallen since—
freshly minted—

and hills marked heavens swelled to one of its windows
        union all around leaves
like Nathan trees
                            and takes along   as she profited
from contribute-behind them
on whether

                  they carry just a few
         as we crossed the homeless kids   among defaults
to old ties to school—and the nineties—
and crackled as we knew this was whispering
in how the humans remember
boil it down time.

You fly   with the creek   and stop
a-gag-restarted-truth-is-returning
and pages have a drink
                                  (a glass line on this one, was it?)

or was it a peach tree growing
in the grand sweet and free?

When you choose to run
these are still loves to offset the loan industry
mosque in the sea breeze to the sun
too-long white.
'Where can you think,' he began,
the stones beneath you

only see this link to the trouble of drinking water.'
Second, it was like these decrees on its bid on the mall
living in policy with some of the rings
and what time, the timeout
stood on the waiting to be known
as close as well as from time to this

and that balance
their own casting agent
and it was time to lead to the saddle
and go
and of all the willing she can sit and
boil it down, Harry

and the rearing instantly to open it
and then the old shades of the line
in the head and time to ship Paestum
rages bring it
into a string,
it was time to put on the highest

and time to stand in this year's show
that lined the weaned up in the enclosure
reaches to be tall
and writing down

without grizzling
and growing regions for green trees,

it was time as never again it was time
to pull off an upset
directing those songs
rescinded from the heel of arms fired up
to where the helpful in what was chopping the most
wins with silver rights for all

boil it down, Harry.

Oracle

What he sees beauty supplying him with
is instructing himself in front of the workflow
addicted to living and the 'that's what you are'
Nike's will timing this and any new toys
expiate the lights and rains fall in lotus leaves, the sun;
Sven Robinson was himself a nationality,
the July issue was talking gripes
boosting it very slow.
Sit back and watch.
The sun was in that movie starring Townsend
as the prince of Denmark,
asking of the new world 'what U.N. delegate
is riding on the only way?'
He's gravity's asylum,
rows into the cockpit
and pennanting above the collection.
Foley and Mitchell, running it,
have had too much of war to accept
and, spreading the way of string,
what is productive is nothing
other than war:
to fall, to watch
the endless pool kittling
above the Hotel SK
which has its own real mortality, despite
the obscure resurrections of its rooms.

Dolly Donato

Write this is all very high calling plan to reveal.
Do not presume to think that wasted project
and I project a dollar plan,
will manage the school into and by the sun.
Long and lasted, that is the line
given the name of god, gives to know
how old is actually typed a landing.
You break some palace and Seymour the Sting
in the UK disclaims my invite for nine:
he tells us he gets by on the land watch
while which was still a city, still
a stand that involves emptying in the sand
winds up through the crumpled tracery,
still stands on cold,
on his cells at the ninth.
Much social detail: his successor finds
what used to run a hassle
to play breach and tragic, that, to dismiss the Knight
he's hit the session,
did not try from Shimizu, has said in effect,
'on sunset confines and his speed is filing crops,' are in his cell
control styles have much faith in the film.
I know it's strange that she too should be in excess
of all the shares, my son, to take his head
from side and got into this:
this is the visible.

Monday is a Z

He stands in the desert museum on this
and has trumpets stand for these actual eyes,
is foundering complete and sneered, called command,
'tell that it's golden well as pensions raid
which yet survive stand on this lot of things.'
The hand that's more than an uptick trade.
And on the pedestal these would simply monitor
of the menus guilty to look on my works.
You might see, understand nothing; beside
reminds me of the decline of the colossal rate
and London metals the level in strange fire away.

Ozymandias

Percy Bysshe Shelley

I met a traveller from an antique land,
Who said—'Two vast and trunkless legs of stone
Stand in the desert. . . . Near them, on the sand,
Half sunk a shattered visage lies, whose frown,
And wrinkled lip, and sneer of cold command,
Tell that its sculptor well those passions read
Which yet survive, stamped on these lifeless things,
The hand that mocked them, and the heart that fed;
And on the pedestal, these words appear:
My name is Ozymandias, King of Kings;
Look on my Works, ye Mighty, and despair!
Nothing beside remains. Round the decay
Of that colossal Wreck, boundless and bare
The lone and level sands stretch far away.'

He Toils

Visitors as if they need never amount
to the old style, with its ranges
at schools and hot fudge truth in Congress
amongst the new machinery and silver
Philippines mill workers' protein is how this time trucks
rolling past a ghostly wimp, greens stalls,
and Chappell's cutting the fixed silo's baffling.
Know what about the harvest field?
Every bean in the farmer was hungry for spies,
now even mentioned bringing the old son
back into service. Is today in the way for as far back
as could be remanded? Since prices by bees this year
and its foundations while waiting to buy kind
sprouted as I leave from the great mass of action,
the sun had pledged the walls by and watch
while the past to the heavily polled dole
was afraid that if a long thin stream of unhealthy blood
before the storm switch through sickly
on summer evenings, red tile, black caucus,
two settled in mind sparking the stroll
like a volcano. Fire opting for the heart
of the whites' island trembling with an educator
encourages could offer and lightning tracking a man's
police highlighted dampen the rupture
with Sunday going out and Patrick Stewart's a farmhouse
where from the console the speaker was on the flight crew
for in the case of the cockpit, two's describing a person
from reaching a peak-parole education release.

Adamant Parenthood Comforts

I can set as genesis, a potato head sense
that his limbs and features were coming unstuck,
the family solutions in the face of AIDS.

Body increases lost can always be reclaimed,
moves reconfigured, Dummett phantoms.
Can moebius waves replace him softly as a toilet?

Many times I think all his French is passive
in the playground, and it changes the lives
that give much attention to the front of the gal he likes.

If she has been installed as consistent, then I say
they have to service fees for the giants
for five to eighteen, that's what might happen.

If reality breaks, also it's found scorching speeches.

Same as a test added his limbs and faces,
and some have found a solution
that site is back in place, as was last
and will always be reclaimed
as a man is registered: Dummett Phantom
and new members would have replaced sales
(the most demanding comments on the mall)
and later, fingers old attention in front of the gulf.
You like so much that she has been installed
as the Miss, and is protected and served as
Master Landmark, to tell surfaces for the games
to provide a team, and a lot like a time in public,
assists the spaces.

Tranced

He was a living legend
until some great structure mailing
consistent about the most of us
who went through the experience
when doctor and one can't talk about the work
of skill and the judges on the squad missed the point.
Was trying to craft a reason for the hot to sell
some city $9 million the defeat of very much?
He got used to five, and how did you really, Michael Lipper,
you were using really a busy still alive would just use.
Live on in the Lincoln reviews. Have to.

And the fact is,
Israel is making a new complex,
training is seeking a factory
and Celine is likely to pass by,
seeking a traffic accident. And after equipping, who
can have a second Dixieland up?
And you'd have to offer services. The other end of adolescence
lights up your magazine.
Isn't it fine, this July to have CNN instruct why
plane rides, subpoenas, popular mysteries
find us like a family?

Rupture is in us

That sentiment is to make and model inflation,
closing activities.
Fictions in these so insistent planes

attack like a threshold,
crossing a console, flattering
through the chamber.

Deliverance is a privilege ritual,
confinement of heritage's class guy
who is full of our times.

The force to attack the thing
is because it is most erotic in my church,
gravel on the altar.

The status of the external canal
in the shell is like a city's mechanical
clearing on Swanson and on Rathdown.

Salt into the stock
assists me in coming to town with
slide bars, PC feed

swollen to the site of existence.

Dead Soviet Stir

Walking around in the park
should feel better than work,
like the sun, Chong,
the crystal island.

Political, a grand voice
is beyond blacks talking. This is
not a bad place to play,
it doesn't say may-

be one of the menu
might have been an option, and
halted results dictate
his share of clocks with the judge's

works. To slash the passion,
still fight from accidents
and characters in long kites
take the lead about skits.

Old coaching, that I would
have a stripper week.
Think of buying them
during the hours, John.

Watching the parade deliver
sun by class, cover
the children dying high
and think of buying them

to any other filings
by some bit of liability
is no way to get the endorsement
for inspecting to tens.

93 million try.
My life had secretary
Marcia allocated.
What else can I answer

when the lights come on out, for
at the end of another you,
give me a multi-tight
help. We can cemetery, right?

Eat My Quin

Mr. Golden Orange Sherbet
in the silky truce
                        clubs and crests over the glory box attacker,
and as I can follow some insidious marriage
     flat on the loans
                   which are sprinkled as tea.

It's a single event in flux—
hoping evidence
                       of an eighteen-minute stew in detail
and tying into the corners
                                  for critical tangles
of love
         with twelve;

however—
if we mentioned there's more to say   than just a lot;
               for example,
the telephone wire-tap or the com ports
up the middle ground of stealing used photographs
     (lots of small beer, Wednesday).

     But that lot of the northwest wing!
Skylarks
            high of cattle get hungry!
Manson goods go drifting into friends
with the sound of most killings
                                        about ten minutes an inch.

We must either profoundly gobble up the night
as coral,
      and say

repeatedly to the face of Sony 'the sport's racial today,'
and will praise Tesco
undistinguished by prime placement.

There's a new love right now!
I can't use whatever is at variance with the cuisine:
warship divorce?
Human order has a house in a query
which is quite different from a nation in its place
with attachments of defensive,

indignant uncle liquid \$8.00
and has lost interest in cash
and strong remorse
with a farmer
has done enough struggling
to survive one day

and the office wrests from Ferry
a lot in short of the high compared course
of their identity
almost in a flash
uses a title as gravity
in a continuous recovery movement.

Pity the high as scissors
continually ranging with address between sessions in unconsciousness,
the sort that makes him say,
'My heart of evolution,
through the pace beneath the fact,
within for quite a bit when the bus of a retention time.'

Some purchase laughing punishment.
Costs

by two people most often on this level
especially when they changed back into the run
and all holiness speaks from the other world of action
and media is interleaved on a continuing plane.

It's hard to fight his way!
Looking into the law should make some small sum grimace,
or not.
More natural to look at the bit
about the straight Las Vegas' greedy peach,
courageous and prudential as any of the script training:

miles of settlement to watch the unceasing
on/off grace
that attends
nearly every move and creams.
Paris has a launching tape
and recovers at the same price.

Movements
in the shapes of trees and complex in the cells
and fellow
workers' receipts indivisible
and scarcely would that let us from the income interval
we sometimes claim,

from being trapped in the point
that minds analysis,
said pointedly, 'Usually available for Grant:
an equally old background
like a painting of the quality of infinite detailed extent.
I can't attention when nothing is diminished by perspective.'

Did Unfathomable Flagrant Pout

(Together into a lot tougher   now   that stuff)

Bridge
            at this critical jelly   made from grapes off the tree
that growing doubts corner   and still grows, it does:

the country and never once   always credible song
that contrary to unflattering   skyways can bristle more quick

for it
        than for it   for granted script
could be a thought!?'   Was that rehire amended the same time,

a pebble of this life   when a case to the staff request
for ships and ole Miss   my eyes were on stalks?

Dollars
            back in an old market cap   *right ;)*
making the rounds of the district,   resting its foxglove,

spelling tab parsley and nettles. Old highs,
summer SmallCap fund: there

are entries
            sending can come   like tough luck
its credit or ten years until hindsight,   honour of gold for now.

My hand respirator found faced as the crowd at the crossroads
with your life has said that taste buds,   and he doesn't know them,

spread the jelly a stake   as if *they* were not tomorrow.

Low Ripe Windfall

The angry crowd at the hungry ridge
must scramble away. Must Milton change?
Forget the single ironwork
that night for Spike, we know we're had.
Land-use: phony, delicate,
and his speech of the flower,
at last surrender mysterious pages
that covers either the gravel plan
like the words of all a girl
of local content.
Could gentler skies say 'Nellie Bly'
and cripple our sacred?
Two weigh the tape-tree
falling on a water lily case,
for me and many another can box spring
where Rob Blake's 'Y', a letter
of the humble lets the gravel times.
All the anger becomes US troops
on to the hard-to-trace hot
that received the woods of a llama.

An Icon-warmer Hit

Intellect would lose the whole
point itself,
in truth, onto the field,
and he comes with new to the growth
of the one hand
like a grateful checking
and checking its mind
that if I want to show the calamity,
that would use compost that still hasn't risen.

Tries to explain it's of this, often
doctors can be a big story
reviewed with them
and brushstrokes are one to say
that reports, and that's what this is.
A script says models from the majors
crippled like a quarterer.

Genie Wanks Fan

River run past.
They've seen the evidence from Swift
and, sure to band of day,
brings his bike and ideas of the console-
free circulation back to health
council and environs,
centrist room of the oil and
I'm all for another short say,
how a person from north
of the Moore account
of the scientists' cranky piece
was the fear of mana and we'll define
his pianist, a solid wall.
'No Head' Thompson was rocked by the strain of corny
exaggerated themselves to Lawrence County
scored two goals while they went gold
and the amount of overtime nor a voice from afar
bellows commission issued to a topic of flood control
not yet over Missouri.
To have the kids get us into the plan
told of set the stage for that Welfare in Venice
he would say, 'see, sisters are off with the coroner',
nothing-to-look-at page of Cosmo
by a client roaring into their Reagan brown
was to be seen ringing some of the aquifer
the fold of a pound, but don't hire the minimum condom.
Components on top of form or school
is what I'll daily in bed unmaid
a lot better will construct a grey colt
of old town subtle
test at the top three and access all
Eastgate herself. Please end

where inches have been laid to rest upon the green
since Devlin's first love's living.

See Fred Shoo Fifty Magic Ties

During your sleeves swing through it
like a black leather strap
the future is that it was linux.
It was so blind in front of a bruised apple pie.
Dura minutes towards the will
go into mistakes in the guise of a line
and this is my thinking for a graceful
and headlined lawmaker.
Another city in front of the leafy Wattmann building
and trees. What supplied the orange against
will work in the distance, running
in the big sleep in just before flying
here awhile. Cripple links stock
as *Telegraph* polls will continue
when she said, 'Wilson and weeks, the mix
and I'm trying organs, and this time,
this kind we have, the China recall roles
at the time I connect to the building
and one of the French calls from my hand
and time will divert instants in the user,
allegedly, as it must have one computer
and the other bill, old England patriots'.
There is pain, like King Clive
owns drinking and cream cheese restaurants
and he's reached trying to get more for thousand sand.

#1 Pubic Hell Hat

Chorae of the health ministers
have done for new settlers
and shipping channels are better
than sniffing Federal antitrust
sunrises unless you can see
the whites of their I-lands.
Somebody is like one of those
tremors of public health in pure
and simple icon, at least one
of our guys became a reflection
like a record set down
and spinning in the enemy
camp. It works out fine
if you're lucky as to where
the country's house takes
some stem cell research:
expect to play for hospitals and
not to sell as if it's an ideal
season when the rains come,
when the giants,
when I try not to do this.

#2 Pubic Hell Hat

How much further can violence be from one?
Some seventh circle sap, some circle the spotlight is
leaving love and dysfunctional relationships
in real time by handouts? We are younger than the old
with hands like lions from bloodletting
and a panel of young females (German tourists)
where next year is volatile and unconstitutional
and shoots at the light, striking through some old guy,
a professional denouncing what he's doing
and he will sell me to talk, though I'm not thinking
and he disapproves, and seems not to matter,
and as the nagging allies of the young are curious
as to why he is the fox software, a spotlight on them
for he will allow us to see it all, and it takes one to tell,
to tell someone they should sustain alternatives
and the old man's land spice girls wait and see
and one skin is a life in the patches that gave the giant
clams to kick, and they recoiled as the patch shifted
like wedding bands with blood on their hands
and they will come, all the objects you have acted
are in place, called up into snow on the ground
and on your watch, watching doubts leap out of engines
as the final act takes over the jolly stench.

I Claim Mug Pun

'Country in the city street
but the children around your feet
should be in the cool world
of leafy forest wools
and wild Coles,' he's saying to me,
like a cork of course
striking broken the thing wrong,
strengthened into quarters
its help prolongs his home hand
and lease listening express is hopeless news.
Municipal down the does
dollars to see those seeking a black cross
of the treatment of fellow students
one of the gun done to us.

Afterword: from voice to myth

In this concluding essay I want to examine the relationship between poetry and science in terms of two strangely interrelated concepts: myth and scientism. For the purposes of this discussion, I distinguish between two aspects of 'myth': the broader sense in which Northrop Frye writes of the operation of the imagination to identify the human with the non-human world (19; Humphries 2); and a narrower sense in which I characterise myth as an assemblage of particular elements, which can therefore be understood as a resource of language. Scientism is that attitude which attends to science like an intellectual cyclops which, in its crudest sense, cannot see that other branches of learning and culture exist (Midgley 150). Scientism is as pervasive as the Christian myth, defining our attitude towards the arts (they 'progress', they conduct 'experiments'), structuring the modern university (including the absurdity of the creative writing 'thesis' and 'exegesis', among other aspects), yet remaining blind to its own standing as a powerful contemporary myth. Myths circulate in a culture through language and through the arts in general; poetry is one influential distiller, formulator and resuscitator of them. In this paper I will examine two myths which have circulated freely between poetry and science, the Gaia hypothesis and atomism, before concluding with a brief discussion of the utility of myth.

The two aspects of myth which I have identified above are obviously inter-related; as a resource of language, however, myth has a number of features that are important to delineate. One is Jean-Luc Nancy's observation, citing Marcel Détienne's *L'Invention de la mythologie* (1981) that 'myth as such is an "unlocatable genre"'; another is that myths are always to hand in the sense that 'we know that although we did not invent the stories … we did on the other hand invent the function of the myths that these stories recount' (45). While Détienne speaks of 'the fleeting, ungraspable essence of myth' (Nancy 159n), it is also readily present for use in poetic invention. Another aspect of myth is that it is often an originary narrative; equally, it can also be foundational or definitional/explanatory.

I am mostly concerned in this essay with the myths that are available to us contemporaneously, and so I am therefore situating my discussion after modernism's engagement with the 'primitive' and in this regard my argument echoes David Macarthur's 'radical hypothesis that modernist art *as a whole* is a Western response to tribal culture. Australasian modernism is to a large but indeterminate extent a Western response to Aboriginal culture.' (228) Indeed, the 'primitive'[10] overshadows our current understanding of myth, so much so that 'myth' is often only conceived of in terms of the ancient, the 'primitive' or the 'original'. Yet there are a number of myths circulating in contemporary Australia which have at least one relatively recent origin: one example is the Ned Kelly story, which is affiliated with the myth of the 'larrikin' as being somehow representative of the Australian national character (a point to which I shall return). In this regard I prefer to see myth as a kind of 'handle', in the sense that it is both definitional (a 'handle' as a person's name) and is something which can be grasped and then used for some purpose.

The last point I would like to make about myth is that it has no single point of origin. 'Origin' here is not to be confused with an historical event or person, such as the crimes and execution of Ned Kelly, around which a myth has been built. The origin of a myth is not derived from an author: 'mythology is not invented by individuals: it has proceeded from the *people* itself' (Schelling 45). If an account of how myth originates is demanded, to this I would respond that any such account would itself be mythic. That is, any explanation for how a myth comes into being is usually itself a kind of originary myth which either supplements or substitutes for the original myth. An example of this is Claude Lévi-Strauss' conceptualization of the 'gross constituent units' of myth, which later came to be termed 'mythemes':

> 1. Myth, like the rest of language, is made up of constituent units.
> 2. These constituent units presuppose the constituent units present in language when analyzed on other levels, namely, phonemes, morphemes, and semantemes, but they, nevertheless, differ from the latter in the same way as they themselves differ from morphemes, and these from phonemes; they belong to a higher

> order, a more complex one. For this reason, we will call them *gross constituent units.* ('Structural Study of Myth' 431)

There is a difference between stating that myth is 'an assemblage of particular elements' and that it is 'made up of constituent elements'. For example, an important element of the Ned Kelly myth is his helmet, yet Ned Kelly's helmet is not a mytheme, as it is not shared or 'bundled' with other related mythemes (Lévi-Strauss *Structural Anthroplogy* 211). The constituent units to which Lévi-Strauss refers are examples of the atomistic myth which came to predominate at the end of the nineteenth century and informed many foundational assumptions in the human sciences throughout the twentieth century (a point to which I shall return below). Having outlined my understanding of myth as a resource of language, I now want to look at the development of the Gaia hypotheis, and specifically its mythic dimensions.

The Gaia hypothesis originated in James Lovelock's 'flash of enlightenment' while he was working in Pasadena California in 1965, that 'life defines and maintains the material conditions needed for its survival', and that the whole planetary ecosystem 'seemed to exhibit the behavior of a single organism-even a living creature' (Lovelock *Quest for Gaia* 304). Lovelock published a brief note in 1968 in *The Proceedings of the American Astronautical Society* and a letter to *Atmospheric Environment* in 1971 before collaborating with the biologist Lynn Margulis in the mid-1970s.

Nomenclature was crucial to the success of Lovelock's ideas in a couple of ways. The first of these is 'Gaia' itself:

> My contemporary and fellow villager, the novelist William Golding, suggested that anything alive deserves a name—what better for a living planet than Gaia, the name the Greeks used for the Earth Goddess? (Lovelock *Ages of Gaia* 3)

William Golding was an avid reader of classical Greek and it is tempting to assume that knowledge of Hesiod was his sole source; certainly, there is no entry at all for Gaia or Gaea in Eric Smith's *A Dictionary of Classical Reference in English Poetry* (1984). However, a look at entries for other goddesses in that work suggests a more complex picture. As Ronald Hutton notes

> Between 1800 and 1940 Venus (or Aphrodite) retains her numerical superiority in appearances with Diana (or Artemis) coming second. Juno, however, almost vanishes, and so does Minerva after 1830. The third place is now taken by Proserpine, as goddess of the changing seasons or of the dead, and the fourth by Ceres or Demeter, lady of the harvest. A reading of the texts listed discloses a much more striking alternative. Venus now appears not merely as patroness of love but related to the woodland or the sea. Diana is no longer primarily a symbol of chastity or hunting, but of the moon, the greenwood, and wild animals. Furthermore, when a goddess is made the major figure in a poem, instead of the subject of an incidental reference, the supremacy of Venus is overturned. Diana now leads, or else a generalized female deity of moonlight or the natural world, most commonly called 'Mother Earth' or 'Mother Nature'. (33)

Diana, therefore, was gradually transformed into the Earth Goddess, fusing also with the figure of Demeter in particular. As the Greek goddess of Earth, Demeter really only begins to appear in English poetry from the second half of the nineteenth century, a little later than the rise of Diana, in the work of poets such as Arnold, Bridges, Lawrence, Meredith, Swinburne and Tennyson (Smith 77). Why should this be?

Broadly speaking, the rise of an Earth Goddess accompanied the nineteenth century progress of industrialisation and scientific discovery. Ronald Hutton's history of modern pagan witchcraft *The Triumph of the Moon* (1999) traces the development of the German Romantic idea, especially in the work of Herder, the Schlegels and Tieck, that prehistoric religion was 'an embodiment of sublime truths, which had degenerated and been forgotten among most modern tribal peoples' (35; 419n). Hutton also examines the development of the idea of a primeval Goddess through many later thinkers across a range of disciplines. For example, in 1849 the classicist Eduard Gerhard 'advanced the novel suggestion that behind the various goddesses of historic Greece stood a single great one, representing Mother Earth and venerated before history began', an idea which was adopted by other classicists such as Ernst Kroker, Fr. Lenormant, and M.J. Menant, and meshed with other theories, such as that of the Swiss judge J.J. Bachofen 'that the earliest human societies had been woman-centred, altering to a patriarchal form before the beginning of history; what was true in the secular sphere should also, logically, have been so in the religious one' (35-6). In 1901 Sir Arthur Evans converted to the idea that 'prehistoric Crete had venerated a single mighty goddess' while excavating Knossos, later associating her with neolithic 'Venuses' and historic Near Eastern goddesses (36). Later figures such as Edmund Chambers, a civil servant and scholar of the medieval stage, classicist Jane Ellen Harrison, anthropologist Sir James Frazer, and archaeologist Joseph Dechelette, among many others, all promoted the idea of a single great goddess as central to prehistoric religious belief; yet Hutton observes of Evans that 'he and the scholars who preceded or followed him had projected backwards upon prehistory the goddess who had emerged as pre-eminent in the minds of poets and novelists during the nineteenth century' and that 'between 1840 and 1940 historians and archaeologists had turned Neolithic spirituality into a mirror of Christianity, but one which emphasized opposite qualities: female instead of male, earth instead of sky, nature instead of civilization' (39-40).

The Great Goddess, therefore, is as much a product of modernity as a response to it, and Golding's contribution to Lovelock's hypothesis is merely one step in a mythopoeic development that also informed the rise of neo-paganism and second wave feminism. Apparently, the flimsiness of the archaeological evidence was no impediment to the hunger for an alternative myth to that of the official culture of the times and to the fact that the resources were readily to hand, in poetry, novels, art and folklore. And it has been a very useful myth.

In his notebooks concerned with anagrams in Saturnian verse, Saussure investigated the transmission of legends (which I take to mean particular instances of myth) across time as a way of understanding how the principle of anagrammatic distribution in Saturnian verse might also be transmitted from generation to generation. Saussure's conception of the legend is close to how I understand myth to be primarily a resource of language. While Saussure assumes, according to Starobinski, that 'historical characters are taken over by legend' (Starobinski 6), he is focused on what is to hand for the

> poet who gathers and organizes legend only recovers, for any particular scene, those things which are *properties* in the most exact, theatrical sense. When the actors have left the stage, a few objects remain: a flower on the floor, a [ ] which lingers in the memory, suggesting more or less what has happened, but which, being only partial, leaves room for –' (Starobinski 7).

Usually this results in 'a profound conservative tendency which dominates the realm of legend', but if there is change, then 'Imagination, *across a memory gap*, is the principal factor' (7).

Where imagination is at work, Saussure sees a kind of 'nobility' which, like that of language, 'lies in the fact that restricted as both are to elements of particular meaning, they then unite these elements, continually drawing new meanings from them.' (8). It is worth looking at detail what Saussure goes on to say about this process:

> A solemn law regulates these processes, which one would do well to consider before concluding that this conception of legend is false: nowhere do things flourish which are not a combination of inert elements, and nowhere can we perceive matter as other than that constant nourishment which thought directs, regulates, and controls, but on which it is dependent.
>
> To imagine that a legend begins with one particular meaning and has since its origin had the meaning it currently enjoys or, conversely, to imagine that it could not have had any meaning whatever is an exercise beyond my powers. It seems to suppose that material elements of the legend have not been conveyed across centuries; that, given five or six basic elements, the meaning will change in the space of a few minutes if I give them for combination to five or six people working independently. (8)

Gaia was imagined into being from what was to hand: the Venus of Willendorf, Diana, Demeter, Persephone, Hecate, Hesiod. The motivation for the myriad imaginings which achieved this is complex, from wanting an inverted form of religious myth in which to believe, to a desire to endow nature with divinity; yet the result is a simple myth which has great utility in addressing global warming.

The second way in which naming was crucial to the success of the Gaia hypothesis was in Lovelock's coining of a new 'discipline' of 'geophysiology' in 1991 (Lovelock, *Gaia: The Practical Science of Planetary Medicine).* According to Mary Midgley,

> when James Lovelock first displayed this idea, the extreme reductivism then prevailing in biology made orthodox scientists reject it outright. Since that time, however, as the details of the idea have been worked out, a good deal of the science involved has been found to be quite plausible and is now being discussed at a normal level. The main difficulty, however, was never about those scientific details. It concerned the imagery, the vision of a wider whole, in some sense a living whole, of which we are a part. It became clear how much this imagery mattered to the scientists when Lovelock introduced a slightly different image, namely the medical model of the earth as a sick planet needing our care and attention – needing, in fact, a science of *geophysiology* to study its health and sickness. (16)

'Geophysiology' is really a myth with a scientific name; we could view it as a para-myth, or even, perhaps, a micro-myth, which I suggest is something which is not quite a myth in its own right but is closely associated with a myth. Whatever we choose to designate it, it is clearly part of a myth which is, and has been, useful to us. By giving a human dimension (other than its cause) to global warming, that it is something which is sickening a female, motherly entity, the formulation of the problem is at once immediately graspable, affecting and powerful. Even if it's a bit daffy, it's a myth worth holding onto for now.

The same cannot be said for the myth of atomism, which is the focus of Mary Midgley's book *Science and Poetry*. Richard Dawkins' idea of 'The Selfish Gene' sits firmly in her cross-hairs, and in particular his notion of the 'meme' as the fundamental unit of which culture is composed (70). Just about anything ending in '-eme' entails the notion of complex systems being ultimately explainable through reduction to fundamental invariant units. There is no mystery to this: Jakobson and Halle contend that in language

> the actual linguistic study of these invariants started only in the 1870's and developed intensively after World War I, side by side with the gradual expansion of the principle of INVARIANCE in the sciences. (2002: 18-19)

As far as I am aware, the 'principle of INVARIANCE' is not a scientific law or a proven fact, and the setting of 'INVARIANCE' in small capitals seems to betray a tacit insecurity. When the 'principle of 'INVARIANCE', is not viewed from the perspective of a social science, in this case of linguistics cosying up to 'the sciences', but from the perspective of poetry, it begins to look suspiciously like a myth: the myth of scientism, built on atomistic foundations.

According to Midgley, Lucretius' poem 'De Rerum Natura' ('On the Nature of Things') 'was the main channel through which the atomic theory of matter reached Renaissance Europe. It was forcibly stated there, all ready to be taken up by the founders of modern physics' (23). While she acknowledges the obvious origin of atomism in Greek philosophical thought, specifically Leucippus and Democritus, the importance of Midgley's identification of Lucretius' influence is what accompanied that idea, specifically the micro-myth of 'true piety' which 'lies rather in the power to contemplate the universe with a quiet mind.' (Book V, lines 1185 and 1194–1203) (25). The myth of atomism is not just a theory of fundamental particles, but is that plus an attack on superstition and religion, those things which get in the way of a 'quiet mind'. The myth of atomism is therefore complex, bringing with it a rejection of any other means of salvation save science. In late Republican Rome, such a myth may have been a novelty, and may also have been provocative; in the nineteenth century, when atomic theory gained its foothold, such a myth was a handy tool of scientism. And according to Midgley, not all myths should be valued equally:

> Obviously the idea of Gaia is a myth, a symbol. But then so is the sociobiological idea of the Selfish Gene. One of these myths emphasises our separateness from the world around us. The other emphasises our profound dependence on it. Since wholes are quite as real as parts, there is no reason in principle why we should have to prefer the first emphasis over the second. The choice between them depends on their relevance to our situation. And given that current situation, there seems to me to be little doubt about which of them we most need to guide our thinking today. (17)

The atomistic myth has served its purpose, aiding in the development of quantum physics, structuralism, and the advent of personal trainers amid much else. Yet physics long ago moved on from the idea of the atom as a 'thing', even if the word is wedged firmly in the popular imagination. It might just have to be the work of poetry to discover a new set of myths so that if the political and social 'sciences' look to physics once more for inspiration, they may be more willing to find a model of the human that is more like a wave than a particle (or, ideally, both).

The relationship between poetry and the sciences is more complex than is usually supposed. Science makes use of myth as much as philosophy does and they often come into science or philosophy from poetry. I've looked at the myth of the Gaia hypothesis and the atomistic basis of scientism, but there are other myths apart from these which are to hand, or could be to hand if we knew where to look. Some of these have potential as yet untapped, while some have passed their use-by date. One myth that is questionable is the Ned Kelly larrikin myth: why does Australian culture so desperately need to hold dear the myth of the rebellious outlaw, the larrikin, the disrespectfully heroic digger, or 'the battler'? Obviously, because it is part of the ongoing process of decolonisation. Yet it can be the work of poetry to bring myth into focus and transform our reality in ways that can be of use in science and in other fields of inquiry. For example, what if the myth of the larrikin were to be replaced with the myth of the tyre-kicker, that we are a nation of tyre-kickers in the used car yard of current ideas? As a foundational fiction it is as appealing as any other contender, even more so as it engenders the scepticism which accompanies the enlightenment discourse upon which modern Australia was founded, and also a skepticism directed towards itself.

If the tyre-kicker can become a foundational myth (and it can: I didn't make it up, it was already to hand), then that scepticism could (and should) be directed to the myth that in Australia there is a near-absence of uniquely Australian myths. On the contrary, the land itself is teeming with them, but mostly we can't hear them. While I have mentioned one that is particular to an Australian Anglo-celtic tradition, there are obviously many others inaccessible through languages lost and through belief systems to which access may not be granted. Yet this perception of 'lack' or absence is not necessarily a particularly Australian problem, nor is it necessarily true. Nancy notes that after modernism, 'everything leads us to a world in which mythic resources are profoundly lacking' (47), although it is clear that Nancy is concerned with myth as Schelling defines it, as 'an operation of engenderment (53) and, as such tends towards conceiving of myth in terms of those of ancient cultures, such as the Greeks'. I would agree that the resources for these myths are indeed scarce, but those for other myths are plentiful. For example, there are communities in Australia which are as much an expression of nationalist myths such as those of Ned Kelly or the larrikin as they are professed believers in their 'truth', and there are other communities for which the myth of 'the market is always right' is a binding and foundational narrative. And there are plenty of others to choose from.

I'd like to conclude on a speculative note a little removed from the theme of poetry and science, but hopefully not wholly irrelevant. As noted earlier, Australian poetry has already tried engaging with indigenous cultures through the 'primitivist' modernism of the Jindyworobak movement (Kirkpatrick 128). The problems of this movement are starkly apparent today and can be summarised by Elazar Barkan and Ronald Bush's observation of primitivism in general that 'as for "primitives", they never existed. Only Western "primitivism" did' (2). Consequently, the mythic elements of Jindyworobakism were viewed or produced wholly through such a primitivist lens. I want to suggest that the learning of indigenous languages be compulsory in Australian schools. Without access to those languages which flourished and developed on this continent for thousands of years, we lack one of the basic transformative tools (and modes) of the imagination which developed here. It is only through this process that we can truly achieve reconciliation, for the establishment or identification of a unique voice in a language is what gives us access to myth (and here I am not at all advocating the appropriation of sacred belief systems, but rather those myths that are a resource to each language). We need, for a while at least, to become all ears.

Notes

1. Quine cites Wilson, 1959, p. 532. Perhaps he had in mind his nephew Robert Quine (1942-2004), guitarist with Richard Hell and the Voidoids, Lou Reed and many others, when thinking of the need to translate 'cool', 'square' and 'hopefully'.

2. Another Australian example of homophonic translation is Afferbeck Lauder's *Strine* books (Lauder, 2009), in which broad Australian is rendered, somewhat phonetically in standard English, yet is defamiliarised through some exaggeration such that it really appears as a heterophonic translation: hence the suitability of the term hetero-homophonic translation here and in later discussion.

3. Bregman notes that this was first proposed by Huggins (1964) and later by Powers and Wilcox (1977).

4. Bregman notes that this suggestion was first made by Cherry and Wiley (1967).

5. A full discussion of these findings and their significance is simply not possible in this book. Nevertheless, such findings need not necessarily discredit Saussure's conception of the arbitrary relation between signifier and sign. It might be that language can be conceived of as a more complex system than that of a purely differential one. From a mereological point of view, it is possible that the relation of part to whole and part to part within a whole is complex and variable (Varzi, 2016).

6. Saussure differentiates between the anagram and the paragram, with the former being a more compressed instance of the latter, which might be spread over several lines (Starobinski, 1979, p. 18).

7. The rules Saussure discerns for his theory of Saturnian verse are complex, and need not be stated in full, although one example can be reproduced as an illustration. Admitting that:

> since it is impossible to state here my theory of Saturnian verse with any completeness, I will cite:
>
> *Taurasia Cīsauna Samnio cēpit*

> This is an anagrammatic line containing the entire name of *Scīpio*, (in the syllables *cī* + *pī* + *ĭō*, in addition to the *S* of Samnio cēpit, which is the first letter of a group in which almost the entire word *Scīpīō* appears – correction of – *cēpi* – by the – *cĭ* of *Cīsauna*). (Saussure in Starobinski, 1979, p. 16)

8. From Saussure's 'Notes inédites':

> The truly ultimate law of language, at least so far as we dare to speak of it, is that there is never anything that can reside in a single term, and this is because of the fact that linguistic symbols have no relation to what they ought to designate, thus that a is incapable of designating something without the help of b, and likewise b without the help of a, or in fact that both of them are without value except through their reciprocal difference, or that neither of the two has value, whether it be through any part of itself (for example, 'the root,' etc.), except by means of the same plexus of eternally negative differences.
>
> It is astonishing. But where in truth would the possibility of the contrary lie? Where would be for a single instant the point of positive irradiation in all language, once granted that there is no vocal image that responds more than any other to what it must say? (as cited in Agamben, 1993, pp. 153-154)

9. I chose 'Cymru' ('Wales' in Welsh) as part of the anagrammatic title to suggest that the notion of 'country' in Mackellar's poem is inescapably based on a northern hemisphere idea of what 'country' can be, while also indirectly referencing 'New South Wales.'

10. Here I am following Macarthur's important qualification: 'I use the terms "primitive" and "primitivism" in a resolutely non-pejorative sense akin to that employed by the MOMA exhibition "Primitivism in 20th Century Art: Affinity of the Tribal and the Modern": "The term 'primitivism' is used to describe the Western response to tribal culture as revealed in the work and thought of modern artists" (MOMA press release, Aug 1984).' (228)

Works Cited

Agamben, G. (1991). *Language and Death: The Place of Negativity.* Translated by K. E. Pinkus & M. Hardt. University of Minnesota Press.

Agamben, G. (1993). *Stanzas. Word and Phantasm in Western Culture.* Translated by Ronald L. Martinez. University of Minnesota Press.

Barkan, Elazar and Ronald Bush. 'Introduction'. *Prehistories of the Future: The Primitivist Project and the Culture of Modernism.* Ed. Elazar Barkan and Ronald Bush. Stanford: Stanford University Press, 1995. 1-19.

Bernstein, C. (2021). *Charles Bernstein: Electronic Poetry Center Author Page.* University of Pennsylvania. Retrieved 12 February 2021, from http://www.writing.upenn.edu/bernstein/experiments.html#:~:text=Homophonic%20translation%3A%20Take%20a%20poem,%22toute%22%20to%20toot)

Blasi, D. E., Wichmann, S., Hammarström, H., Stadler, P. F. & Christiansen, M. H. (2016). Sound-meaning association biases evidenced across thousands of languages. *PNAS*, 113(39). https://doi.org/10.1073/pnas.1605782113

Bregman, A. (1994). *Auditory Scene Analysis: The Perceptual Organization of Sound.* MIT Press.

Cavarero, A. (2005). *For More than One Voice: Toward a Philosophy of Vocal Expression.* Translated by P. A. Kottman. Stanford University Press.

Chambers, R. (2018). Significant others, or textual congress: Concerning Baudelaire and Tranter. *Australian Journal of French Studies,* 55(3), pp. 223-236.

Cherry, C. & Wiley, R. (1967). Speech communication in very noisy environments. *Nature (London)*, 214, p. 1164. https://www.nature.com/articles/2141164a0.pdf

Détienne M 1981 *L'Invention de la mythologie,* Paris: Gallimard.

Frye, N 1947 *Fearful Symmetry: A Study of William Blake,* Princeton: Princeton UP.

Dingemanse, M., Blasi, D. E., Lupyan, G., Christiansen, M. H. & Monaghan, P. (2015). Arbitrariness, iconicity, and systematicity in language. *Trends in Cognitive Sciences*, 19(20), pp. 603-615. https://doi.org/10.1016/j.tics.2015.07.013

Dolar, M. (2006). *A Voice and Nothing More.* MIT Press.

Edwards, C. (2005). A Fluke. *Jacket*, 29. Retrieved 27 January 2020, from http://jacketmagazine.com/29/fluke00intro.shtml

Farrell, M. (2015). *Writing Australian Unsettlement: Modes of Poetic Invention 1796-1945.* Palgrave Macmillan.

Fitch, T. (2019). Aussi / Or: *Un Coup de dés* and Mistranslation in the Antipodes. *Cordite*, 5. Retrieved 27 January 2020, from http://cordite.org.au/wp-content/uploads/2019/05/AUSSI_OR-CORDITE-TOBY-FITCH.pdf

Frye, N. (1947). *Fearful Symmetry: A Study of William Blake.* Princeton University Press.

Glock, H. J. (1993). The indispensability of translation in Quine and Davidson. *The Philosophical Quarterly*, 43(171), pp. 194-209. Humphries, R 1998 'Something Critical is Mything: Identity and Intertext in Northrop Frye' *Colloquy*, (2), 20–29. https://search.informit.org/doi/10.3316/informit.642228325172966 (accessed 14 May 2021)

Griffiths, T. L. (2011). Rethinking language: How probabilities shape the words we use. *PNAS*, 108(10). https://doi.org/10.1073/pnas.1100760108

Heaney, S. (2006). *District and Circle.* Faber and Faber.

Henkel, A. & Schöne, A. (1996). *Emblemata: Handbuch zur Sinnbildkunst Des XVI. und XVII. Jahrhunderts.* Metzler.

Horáček, J. (2014). Pedantry and play: The Zukofsky Catullus. *Com parative Literature Studies*, 51(1), pp. 106-131. https://www.muse.jhu.edu/article/542427

Huggins, A 1964, 'On Perceptual Integration of Dichotically Alternated

Pulse Trains', Journal of the Acoustical Society of America, 56, 939-943

Hutton, R 1999 *The Triumph of the Moon: A History of Modern Pagan Witchcraft,* Oxford: Oxford UP.

Jakobson, R. (1985). *Verbal Art, Verbal Sign, Verbal Time.* Basil Blackwell.

Jakobson, R. & Halle, M. (2002). *Fundamentals of Language* (2nd ed.). Mouton de Gruyter.

Jakobson, R. & Jones, L. (1970). *Shakespeare's Verbal Art in Th'Expence of Spirit.* Mouton de Gruyter.

Jones, B. (2010). *The Last Poems of D.H. Lawrence: Shaping a Late Style.* Ashgate.

Kirkpatrick, P 2013 '"Fearful Affinity": Jindyworobak Primitivism' in P Butterss (ed) *Adelaide: A Literary City,* Adelaide: University of Adelaide Press.

Lauder, A. (2009). *Strine: The Complete Works of Afferbeck Lauder.* Text.

Leithauser, B. (2006). Wild Irish: 'District and Circle'. Review of Seamus Heaney, District and Circle. *The New York Times.* Retrieved 12 February 2021, from https://www.nytimes.com/2006/07/16/books/review/16leithouser.html

Lévi-Strauss, C 1963 *Structural Anthropology,* Trans. Claire Jacobson and Brooke Grundfest Schoepf New York: Basic Books.

Lévi-Strauss, C 1988 *The Jealous Potter,* Trans Bénédicte Chorier Chicago: Chicago UP.

Lévi-Strauss, C 1955 'The Structural Study of Myth.' *The Journal of American Folklore,* vol. 68, no. 270, pp. 428–444. *JSTOR,* www.jstor.org/stable/536768. (accessed 23 May 2021). 431

Lovelock, J 1991 *Gaia: The Practical Science of Planetary Medicine,* North Sydney: Allen & Unwin.

Lovelock, J and Epton, S 1975 'The Quest for Gaia', *New Scientist* 65.

Lovelock, J 1988*The Ages of Gaia: A Biography of Our Living Earth,* Oxford: Oxford UP.

Macarthur, D 2015 'The Experience of Aboriginality in the Creation of the Radically New: On Modernism in Australasian Art', in A Lindgren and S Ross (eds) *The Modernist World,* Melbourne: Routledge, 227–234.

Mackellar, D. (1987). *My Country and Other Poems.* Viking O'Neil.

MacNeice, L. (2001). *Poems Selected by Michael Longley.* Faber and Faber.

Midgley, M. (2001). *Science and Poetry.* Routledge.

Monaghan, P., Shillcock, R. C., Chr istiansen, M. H. & Kirby, S. (2014). How arbitrary is language? *Philosophical Transactions of the Royal Society B*, 369(1651). http://dx.doi.org/10.1098/rstb.2013.0299

Muldoon, P. (2001). *Poems 1968-1998.* Faber and Faber.

Musgrave, D. (2016) *Anatomy of Voice.* GloriaSMH Press.

Musgrave, D. (2019). *Numb and Number.* Puncher & Wattmann.

Musgrave, D. (2021). Paris, capital of the Australian poetic avant-garde: Christopher Brennan's 'Musicopoematographoscope', John Tranter's 'Desmond's Coupé', and Chris Edwards' 'A Fluke' and *After Naptime.* In Rolls, A & Johnson, M. (Eds.), *Remembering Paris in Text and Film.* Intellect.

Nancy, J-L 1991 *The Inoperative Community,* Trans Peter Connor, Lisa Garbus, Michael Holland, and Simona Sawhney Minneapolis: University of Minnesota Press.

O'Leary, A. & Rhodes, G. (1984). Cross-modal effects on visual and auditory objects perception. *Perception & Psychophysics*, 35, pp. 565-569.

Powers, G. & Wilcox, J. (1977). Intelligibility of temporally interrupted speech with and without intervening noise. *Journal of the Acoustical Society of America,* 61, pp. 195-199.

Quine, W. V. (1969). *Ontological Relativity and Other Essays.* Columbia University Press.

Rogues de Fursac, J. & Rosanoff, A. (1905). *Manual of Psychiatry.* Wiley. https://babel.hathitrust.org/cgi/pt?id=mdp.39015070984839&view=1up&seq=71&skin=2021 accessed 7/10/21

Schelling, F 2007 *Historical-critical Introduction to the Philosophy of Mythology*, Trans M Richey and M Zisselsberger New York: SUNY Press.

Shannon, C. E. (1948). A mathematical theory of communication. *The Bell System Technical Journal*, 27(3), pp. 379-423.

Smith, E 1984 *A Dictionary of Classical Reference in English Poetry*, Cambridge: D.S. Brewer

Starobinski, J. (1979). *Words upon Words: The Anagrams of Ferdinand de Saussure*. Translated by O. Emmet. Yale University Press.

Stewart, S. (2009). Rhyme and Freedom. In Perloff, M & Dworkin, C. (Eds.), *The Sound of Poetry/The Poetry of Sound* (pp. 29-48). Chicago University Press.

Tranter J. (1990). *Selected Poems*. Hale & Iremonger.

Tranter, J. (1998). Mr Rubenking's 'Breakdown'. *Jacket*, 4. Retrieved 10 February 2021, from http://jacketmagazine.com/04/rubenking.html

Tranter, J. (2009). *Distant Voices* [Doctoral thesis, University of Wollongong]. University of Wollongong Thesis Collection 1954-2016. https://ro.uow.edu.au/theses/3191/

Varzi, A. (2016). Mereology. In *Stanford Encyclopedia of Philosophy*. Retrieved 10 October 2020, from https://plato.stanford.edu/entries/mereology

White, W. A. (1911). *Outlines of Psychiatry* (3rd ed.). Nervous and Mental Disease Publishing Company. https://babel.hathitrust.org/cgi/pt?id=chi.55570964&view=1up&seq=32 accessed 7/10/21

Wilson, N. L. (1959). Substances without substrata. *Review of Metaphysics*, 12(4), pp. 521-539.

Wright, J. (1996). *A Human Pattern: Selected Poems*. Imprint.

Zukofsky, C. & Zukofsky, L. (1991). *Catullus (Gai Valeri Catulli Veronensis Liber)*. Translated by Zukofsky, C & Zukofsky, L. In *Complete Short Poetry*. Johns Hopkins University Press.

Acknowledgements

An earlier version of 'Pubic Hell Hat #1' was highly commended in the Gwen Harwood Poetry Prize. An earlier version of the introductory essay was first published as 'Mishearing and the Voice in Poetry' in *Text* 25 (special issue 64) 01 Jan 2021. An earlier version of the afterword was first published as 'Poetry as Speculative Science: the origins of the Gaia hypothesis in poetry and myth' in *Axon: Creative Explorations* 11(1):9 pages 01 Jul 2021.

Thanks to John Watson, Todd Turner for reading this book in its proof stages and making useful editorial suggestions.

Printed in Australia
Ingram Content Group Australia Pty Ltd
AUHW021148021023
384392AU00004B/4

9 780645 801903